W9-CLC-447

9/08

THE STORY OF THE
KANSAS CITY ROYALS

SEC. **14**
ROW **8**
SEAT **10**

GRANDSTAND SEAT $6.00
Est. Price $5.00 • Tax $1.00 • TOTAL

GAME **4**

Right hereby reserved to refund said price
and revoke license granted by this ticket.

DAY GAME
THE BALLPARK
★ ★
American League
vs.
National League

GAME **4**

Read Important
Notices on
Reverse Side
★
Do Not Detach
This Coupon From
Rain Check

RAIN CHECK

DAY GAME
GRANDSTAND SEAT
Est. Price $5.00 $6.00
Fed. Tax $1.00
TOTAL
Right hereby reserved to re-
fund said price and revoke
license granted by this ticket.

READ IMPORTANT NOTICES
ON REVERSE SIDE

GAME **4**

SEC. **14**
ROW **8**
SEAT **10**

Published by Creative Education
P.O. Box 227, Mankato, Minnesota 56002
Creative Education is an imprint of The Creative Company

Design and production by Blue Design
Printed in the United States of America

Photographs by Corbis (Bettmann), Getty Images (Bernstein Associates, Bruce Bennett Studios, Peter Brouillet, Jeff Carlick/MLB Photos, Jonathan Daniel, Jonathan Daniel/Allsport, Diamond Images, Focus on Sport, Otto Greule Jr, Jeff Hixon, Jim McIsaac, National Baseball Hall of Fame Library/MLB Photos, Rich Pilling/MLB Photos, Jamie Squire, Jamie Squire/ALLSPORT, Rick Stewart, Rick Stewart/Stringer, Ron Vesely/MLB Photos, Tim Umphrey/TUSP)

Copyright © 2008 Creative Education
International copyright reserved in all countries.
No part of this book may be reproduced in any form without written permission from the publisher.

Library of Congress Cataloging-in-Publication Data

Gilbert, Sara.
The story of the Kansas City Royals / by Sara Gilbert.
p. cm. — (Baseball: the great American game)
Includes index.
ISBN-13: 978-1-58341-490-3
1. Kansas City Royals (Baseball team)—History—Juvenile literature. I. Title. II. Series.

GV875.K3G55 2007
796.357'6409778411—dc22   2006027466

First Edition
9 8 7 6 5 4 3 2 1

Cover: Pitcher Bret Saberhagen
Page 1: Third baseman George Brett
Page 3: Outfielder David DeJesus

THE STORY OF THE
KANSAS CITY ROYALS

by Sara Gilbert

HA

CASS COUNTY PUBLIC LIBRARY
400 E. MECHANIC
HARRISONVILLE, MO 64701

0 0022 0327239 4

Kansas City Royals

With Kansas City holding an 11-run lead in the top of the ninth inning at Royals Stadium, Royals third baseman George Brett knew that within moments, his team would officially defeat the St. Louis Cardinals in Game 7 of the 1985 World Series—and he wanted to celebrate the occasion appropriately. So after the second out was made, Brett jogged to the mound, where 21-year-old pitcher Bret Saberhagen was eager to finish his five-hit shutout and take home the trophy. "Stay on the mound after the third out," Brett told young "Sabes," who happily agreed. Moments later, when Royals right fielder Darryl Motley caught a fly ball for the final out, Brett ran toward the mound again, faster this time, and leapt into Saberhagen's arms for an enthusiastic embrace that seemed to capture all of the emotion the rest of the Royals players and Kansas City fans were feeling as well. For the first time in team history, the Royals were baseball's world champions.

ROYALS RISING

Kansas City, Missouri, sits squarely in the middle of America's heartland and has been an important location in the history of the United States. Famed explorers Meriwether Lewis and William Clark passed through on their journey to the Pacific Ocean. It served as a gateway for pioneers making their way west along the Oregon, California, and Santa Fe trails. And it was the original home of Hallmark Cards and the birthplace of barbecue.

In 1969, the city celebrated another new birth: the Kansas City Royals, an American League (AL) expansion team brought to town just two years after the Athletics, the hometown team since 1955, had relocated to Oakland, California. The Royals confidently entered Municipal Stadium for the first time on April 8, and 25-year-old center fielder Lou Piniella promptly led the game off with a solid double to left. Piniella, whose fiery temperament was softened by his sweet swing, went on to score the first run in Kansas City's first win and earned 1969 AL Rookie of the Year honors with a .282 batting average. Piniella's hustle at the plate and in the outfield helped the team put together a 69–93 record—the best showing of the four major-league expansion teams that debuted that year.

MUNICIPAL STADIUM – The Royals' first home field had previously been home to four other baseball teams—the Negro League Monarchs, the minor-league Blues, and the major-league Athletics. The Royals spent their first four seasons in the aging stadium.

In 1971, the Royals enjoyed their first winning season and finished in second place in the AL Western Division. Although they took a couple of steps backward in 1972, they started 1973 with a winning attitude. They had just moved into Royals Stadium, their new state-of-the-art home that replaced rickety old Municipal Stadium. With fan favorite Cookie Rojas at second, speedy Freddie Patek at shortstop, and slick-fielding Amos Otis in center, the team looked ready to take off. And then, on August 2, Kansas City brought up a 20-year-old third baseman who would exceed even the wildest expectations of Royals management and fans—George Brett.

By the time Brett joined the team, the Royals were already 62–48 and well on their way to a second-place finish. Over the next few years, Brett helped lead the Royals' charge to the very top of the division. In 1976, he won his first AL batting crown with a .333 average, and the team captured its first division title with 90 wins. Kansas City then took on the heavily favored New York Yankees in the 1976 AL Championship Series (ALCS). Despite Royals pitcher Paul Splittorff's remarkable relief appearance to save Game 2 and Brett's three-run home run in Game 5, the Royals fell to the Yankees in the end, losing the series three games to two.

The Royals did their best to overcome the domineering Yanks the follow-

SATCHEL PAIGE

THE ORIGINAL ROYALTY

Long before the Kansas City Royals played their first game, another royal family had called the city home: the Kansas City Monarchs, charter members of the Negro National League (NNL) in 1920. The Monarchs, whose golden crown logo was quite similar to that of the Royals today, played a total of 37 seasons in the Negro Leagues, making it the longest-running franchise in league history. And in that long history, the team sent more players into major league baseball than any other Negro League team— including second baseman Jackie Robinson (the first ballplayer to break baseball's color barrier), pitcher Satchel Paige, and first baseman Ernie Banks. The Monarchs, whose more than a dozen championships earned them comparisons to the New York Yankees, played in the NNL until it disbanded in 1930; after "barnstorming" (touring the country as an independent team without a league affiliation) for most of the 1930s, the Monarchs became a charter member of the Negro American League (NAL) in 1937. The NAL dissolved in 1962, but the Monarchs continued playing for three more years before officially disbanding. The team's long history, and the history of the Negro Leagues in America, is now celebrated at the Negro League Baseball Museum, which is fittingly located in Kansas City.

PITCHER · BRET SABERHAGEN

When Bret Saberhagen joined the Royals' starting rotation in 1984, he was just 20 years old. But despite his youth, he showed remarkable poise and control, which would become hallmarks of his 16-year major-league career. He won 10 games that first season and doubled that in 1985, when he became the youngest player to win the Cy Young Award and was named the series MVP in the Royals' World Series victory over the St. Louis Cardinals. Saberhagen played for eight years with the Royals and was inducted into the team's Hall of Fame in 2005.

BRET SABERHAGEN
PITCHER

KANSAS CITY
ROYALS

STATS

Royals seasons: 1984–91

Height: 6-1

Weight: 195

- **3-time All-Star**

- **167 career wins**

- **2-time Cy Young Award winner**

- **1,715 career strikeouts**

ing year. In 1977, Kansas City cruised to its second straight division title with a franchise-best 102–60 record and then faced New York again in the ALCS. The Royals' two victories came courtesy of the fine play of designated hitter Hal McRae and pitcher Dennis Leonard, but the Yankees again won three games to return to the "Fall Classic."

The same story played out in 1978. The Royals had a remarkable regular season, winning the AL West for the third consecutive year. Leonard logged 21 wins, and Brett led the league with 45 doubles. But the team could muster only one playoff win in yet another Yankees confrontation, a 10–4 victory in Game 2 of the ALCS. Even so, the team put a positive spin on the experience. "We didn't look at losing to the Yankees as a big defeat," second baseman Frank White later said. "We looked at it as a steppingstone to the future."

However, the next season ended up being a small step backward for the Royals. Brett led the league with 212 hits and 20 triples, and left fielder Willie Wilson paced all big-leaguers with 83 stolen bases, but the 1979 team finished behind the California Angels in the AL West, out of the playoffs for the first time in four years. Royals manager Whitey Herzog was then fired and replaced by Jim Frey.

CATCHER · DARRELL PORTER

Darrell Porter's four seasons with the Royals were the best of his 17-year big-league career. The strong-armed catcher became a fan favorite for his intensity on the field. He routinely recorded one of the highest percentages of base runners thrown out and, in 1979, became just the second catcher in history to tally 100 walks, runs, and RBI in a season. He may be best known, however, as one of the first professional athletes to publicly admit to a substance abuse problem, checking himself into a rehabilitation center in 1980. Although he worked hard to overcome his addiction, it claimed his life in 2002.

DARRELL PORTER
CATCHER

KANSAS CITY
ROYALS

STATS

Royals seasons: 1977–80

Height: 6-0

Weight: 193

- **4-time All-Star**

- **188 career HR**

- **1,369 career hits**

- **826 career RBI**

HAL McRAE

Hal McRae was one of the AL's top designated hitters, batting .300 or better in 7 of his 15 Royals seasons.

CROWNING ACHIEVEMENT

rey's goal in his first season as skipper was to exact revenge on the team that had continually stymied the Royals—the Yankees. His players were happy to help: Wilson led the league in hits (230), runs scored (133), and triples (15), while long-armed reliever Dan Quisenberry tallied the most saves (33). But the most impressive performance was that of AL Most Valuable Player (MVP) George Brett, whose .390 batting average easily topped the league and, for a time, looked like it might top .400—a feat that had not been accomplished since Boston Red Sox great Ted Williams did it in 1941. Although Brett was the biggest star of the season, it was the team as a whole that gave Royals fans a season to remember. "I know I've captured a lot of media attention this past season," Brett told reporters after getting his award, "but the Royals have a team built on teamwork, not on individuals."

The Royals finished the 1980 season 97–65 and, as expected, found themselves facing the Yankees in the ALCS. Kansas City won the first two games thanks to its fine pitching. Game 3, held at venerable Yankee Stadium, appeared to be going to the Yankees, who were clinging to a 2–1 lead in the top of the seventh. But then, with two men on base, Brett blasted a

DAN QUISENBERRY – Quisenberry combined pinpoint control with a "submarine" throwing style to become one of baseball's most dominant closers. Rarely issuing a walk, he led the AL in saves five times in the six seasons between 1980 and 1985.

FIRST BASEMAN · MIKE SWEENEY

Everything changed when Mike Sweeney switched from catcher to first base in 1999. He struggled defensively at first (committing 12 errors in just 74 games) but his power hitting took off. After hitting 8 home runs in 1998, he suddenly slugged 22 balls out of the park and led the team with a .322 average. He followed that up with a career-best year in 2000, hitting 29 homers, driving in 144 runs, and making the first of five All-Star Game appearances. Despite often being named in trade talks, through 2007, Sweeney had spent his entire career with the Royals.

MIKE SWEENEY
FIRST BASEMAN

KANSAS CITY
ROYALS

STATS

Royals seasons: 1995–present

Height: 6-3

Weight: 220

• **5-time All-Star**

• **.304 career BA**

• **190 career HR**

• **799 career RBI**

Goose Gossage pitch deep into the third tier of seats in the outfield stands. "I remember the crack of the bat. The noise of the bat, it was like nothing I had ever heard before," Gossage said. "I will never forget that crack. And then the silence."

That majestic home run quieted the Yankees' fans and sent the jubilant Royals to the World Series, where they met the Philadelphia Phillies. Unfortunately, it was the Royals' fans who were ultimately silenced this time. Kansas City lost the first two games in Philadelphia before heading home. Brett's solo home run in the first inning of Game 3 sparked the team to a 4–3 victory, and Royals first baseman Willie Aikens hit two long balls to help win Game 4. But those would be the only wins for Kansas City; Philadelphia won Games 5 and 6 to take home the trophy.

There would be no second chance at a championship in the strike-shortened 1981 season. The Royals lost 30 of their first 50 games, and Frey was fired shortly after the strike ended. Under his replacement, Dick Howser, the Royals won 20 of their last 33 games and finished ahead of the Oakland Athletics. But when the two teams met in the AL Division Series (ALDS), Oakland swept Kansas City in three games.

Although Wilson led the league with a .332 average, McRae topped the AL with 133 runs batted in (RBI), and Quisenberry notched 35 saves, 1982 also ended in disappointment for the Royals, who went 90–72 but missed the

AMOS OTIS

Amos Otis did all he could to lift the
Royals in the 1980 World Series,
batting .478 and bopping three homers.

SECOND BASEMAN · FRANK WHITE

Frank White had the tall task of replacing the immensely popular Cookie Rojas at second base in 1973. But by the time his 18-year tenure with Kansas City ended, White had also earned the love and respect of the fans. He was an exceptional fielder who played 62 straight errorless games in 1977 and collected eight Gold Glove awards for his defense.

Although he was never known as a power hitter, he twice hit 22 home runs and drove in 886 runs in his career. After retiring in 1990, White stayed with the organization as a coach and minor-league manager.

FRANK WHITE
SECOND BASEMAN

KANSAS CITY
ROYALS

STATS

Royals seasons: 1973–90

Height: 5-11

Weight: 170

- **8-time Gold Glove winner**

- **5-time All-Star**

- **Uniform number (20) retired by Royals**

- **Royals Hall of Fame inductee (1995)**

playoffs. The following year looked promising until four Royals players were charged with attempting to purchase cocaine. The team, which had been on pace for a winning year, finished 20 games out of first with a 79–83 record.

The 1984 season started with several new names on the roster, including Bret Saberhagen, a 20-year-old pitcher who had notched 18 wins in the Royals' farm system the previous year. Although the young phenom hadn't been selected until the 19th round of the 1982 draft, his pinpoint control and surprising maturity quickly earned him a spot in the Royals' rotation. As a rookie, he won 10 games and helped lead the Royals back to a division title with an 84–78 record. Although the Detroit Tigers powered past the Royals in the playoffs, Saberhagen's heroics on the mound reenergized the Kansas City faithful.

Several Royals players posted big numbers in 1985: Wilson ripped 21 triples, and Quisenberry notched 37 saves. But the biggest surprise was Saberhagen, who, at the tender age of 21, won 20 games and became the youngest player ever to win the coveted Cy Young Award as the league's best pitcher. His teammates were as impressed as the rest of the league. "I was always amazed not only by the velocity of his fastball but by the command of his fastball," fellow Royals pitcher Mark Gubicza said. Saberhagen's precision helped put the Royals back in the playoffs, where they met the Toronto Blue Jays in the first best-of-seven ALCS. Kansas City started

WILLIE WILSON

slow but finished strong, coming back from a three-games-to-one deficit to win the series and gain entrance to the World Series.

The 1985 World Series was nicknamed "the I-70 Series," after the interstate linking Kansas City to its opponents, the St. Louis Cardinals. Although the series started on the Kansas City side, the Royals fell behind three games to two and were on the brink of elimination by the time the series returned to Kansas City for Game 6. The Cardinals had a 1–0 lead in the ninth and were ready to celebrate when the Royals got a much-needed break: leadoff hitter Jorge Orta was called safe on a close play at first, although replays showed he was out. The controversial call infuriated the St. Louis dugout and set up a two-run, game-winning rally for the Royals that pushed the series to a seventh game. And that gave Saberhagen the opportunity to win the series for Kansas City. Before a crowd of more than 41,000, he pitched a masterful shutout that finally ended 11–0. The young pitcher, whose first son had been born the night before, was then named series MVP. "What more can I ask for?" Saberhagen said. "It's like the world's at my feet."

Willie Wilson would frequently hit ground balls, beat the throw to first base, and then promptly steal second.

THIRD BASEMAN · GEORGE BRETT

As a 20-year-old rookie in 1973, George Brett thought he knew what a Hall-of-Famer looked like: Carl Yastrzemski. So Kansas City's young third baseman modeled his batting stance after the Boston Red Sox's star outfielder. Twenty-one years later, when Brett retired with a .305 lifetime batting average, it was his posture that younger players were imitating. Brett, who spent his entire career with the Royals and came to epitomize the franchise, was the first player in major-league history to total more than 3,000 hits, 300 home runs, 600 doubles, 100 triples, 1,500 RBI, and 200 stolen bases.

GEORGE BRETT
THIRD BASEMAN

KANSAS CITY
ROYALS

STATS

Royals seasons: 1973–93

Height: 6-0

Weight: 200

- **13-time All-Star**

- **3,154 career hits**

- **317 career HR**

- **Baseball Hall of Fame inductee (1999)**

THE PINE TAR PROBLEM

The Royals trailed the New York Yankees, 4–3, with two outs in the top of the ninth on July 24, 1983. Yankees ace Goose Gossage was on the mound, and Kansas City slugger George Brett was at the plate—a classic matchup of longtime rivals. Brett slammed a two-run homer into the stands, scoring the go-ahead run as he crossed home plate. But just after Brett disappeared into the dugout, Yankees manager Billy Martin stepped out of his and approached the plate. Moments later, home plate umpire Tim McClelland requested Brett's bat. He and the rest of the umpiring crew conferred, then abruptly called Brett out: the pine tar (a substance used to improve grip) on the handle of his bat, they said, exceeded the 18-inch limit. A furious Brett stormed out of the dugout, his eyes bulging. His teammates had to physically restrain the normally mild-mannered player, who was immediately ejected. An appeal to AL president Lee MacPhail reversed the call, on the grounds that "games should be won and lost on the playing field, not through technicalities of the rules." The two teams were forced to finish the game again on August 18 in New York; this time, the Royals really won, 5–4.

BO JACKSON

Bo Jackson's first major-league home run (in 1986) traveled 475 feet, setting a Royals Stadium record.

THE BRETT AND BO SHOW

That euphoric feeling didn't last long. The next season was a disappointment for the Royals, whose 76–86 record—the team's first losing mark in four years—told only part of the story. Manager Dick Howser was diagnosed with a cancerous brain tumor just after the All-Star break. Although he tried to come back after surgery in 1987, by March his illness had forced him to resign. The Royals managed to win 83 games in 1987, but they lost their leader when Howser died in June.

The team's heartache was only slightly tempered by the emergence of several young players—most notably Bo Jackson, a Heisman Trophy winner (as college football's best player) who chose to play pro baseball rather than football after college. In 1987, the muscle-bound outfielder demonstrated his immense talent by hitting 22 home runs but also irritated Royals management by announcing that he was signing with the Los Angeles Raiders to play football "as a hobby." His two-sport status didn't seem to affect his ability to perform, however. In 1988, he hit 25 home runs and helped the team finish third in the AL West. When Jackson led the team with 32 homers in 1989, Kansas City improved to second place. Then an injury slowed Jackson's production, and

SEASON OF SUCCESS

The Royals had already experienced 10 winning seasons, captured six division crowns, and played in one World Series when the 1985 campaign began. They had a feeling that this would finally be their year—although they would have to dig deep to get there. The regular season was a dance between the Royals and California Angels, who kept things interesting right up to the end. But finally, in the second-to-last game, the Royals clinched the crown with a 5–4 victory over Oakland. Their celebration didn't last long, however. Kansas City was routed 6–1 in Game 1 of the ALCS against the Toronto Blue Jays, and Dan Quisenberry blew a save in Game 2. The Royals came back to win Game 3 but lost again in Game 4 to fall behind three games to one. That meant that Kansas City had to win all of the last three games. Although the odds were against them, the Royals did just that and went on to face the St. Louis Cardinals in the World Series. Once again, they fell behind three games to one before rallying to win the final three contests and become world champions at last.

SHORTSTOP · FREDDIE PATEK

At 5-foot-5, Freddie Patek was the smallest major-league player of his time. But the talented shortstop, whose stature earned him the nickname "The Flea," never let height get in the way of stopping a sharply hit ball or firing accurate throws across the field. He had remarkable range, a strong arm, and cat-like reflexes that made him adept at turning double plays in the field; he executed more than 1,000 in his career. Although not a power hitter, Patek had speed on his side; he led the AL with 11 triples in 1971 and 53 stolen bases in 1977.

FREDDIE PATEK
SHORTSTOP

KANSAS CITY
ROYALS

STATS

Royals seasons: 1971–79

Height: 5-5

Weight: 148

- **3-time All-Star**

- **385 career stolen bases**

- **490 career RBI**

- **Hit for the cycle (a single, double, triple, and HR in the same game) on July 9, 1971**

SEASON OF SADNESS

Tears rolled down from behind Dick Howser's trademark sunglasses as he gathered his players for a team meeting at the end of February 1987. "I can't do it," he told them. After two surgeries to remove a tumor found in his brain during the 1986 season, Howser had tried valiantly to return to the team for the 1987 season. But just three days into spring training, it became clear that the popular manager, who had accumulated 404 wins during his six-year tenure with the team, no longer had the stamina to continue. So he resigned, passing the reins to Billy Gardner, who led the team to a second-

place finish in the AL West in 1987. Unfortunately, Howser didn't live to see the end of that season. On June 17, at the age of 51, Howser passed away. On July 3, his uniform number, 10, became the first number retired in Royals history, and Howser was inducted into the team's Hall of Fame. By the end of the year, the Dick Howser Trophy, college baseball's equivalent to football's Heisman Trophy, had been established, and Howser's alma mater, Florida State University, had renamed its field in honor of his contributions to their baseball program.

the Royals suddenly plummeted to 75–86 the following year.

When Jackson's career with the Royals ended after he suffered a serious football injury prior to the 1991 season, the Royals were desperate for new talent. Promising young right-handed pitcher Kevin Appier tallied 13 wins in 1991, while closer Jeff Montgomery earned 33 saves with an arsenal of pitches that included a devastating slider. "We called it the 'manhole slider,'" fellow Royals pitcher Mike Boddicker said. "He threw it up there and it disappeared down a manhole." Still, the 1991 Royals barely topped .500, with an 82–80 mark.

As Kansas City's 1992 campaign came to a close, so did George Brett's quest for 3,000 hits. On September 30, the Royals' revered third baseman became only the 22nd player in history to join the 3,000-hits club. But after two decades in the game, his offensive production was starting to wane. In 1993, as his team put together a respectable 84–78 record, the future Hall-of-Famer announced that he would be retiring from baseball. "I could have played another year, but I would have been playing for the money," Brett said. "Baseball deserves better than that."

GEORGE BRETT

LEFT FIELDER · WILLIE WILSON

Willie Wilson is widely considered the fastest Royals player ever—perhaps the fastest in the majors as well. Of his 802 base-stealing attempts, he slid in safely 668 times, including a league-leading 83 times in 1979. But speed wasn't the talented outfielder's only gift; Wilson picked up a Gold Glove award in 1980, won an AL batting title with a .332 average in 1982, and played in two All-Star Games. Although his reputation was tarnished by drug charges in 1983, Wilson's 15 years with the Royals earned him a spot in the team Hall of Fame in 2000.

STATS

Royals seasons: 1976–90

Height: 6-3

Weight: 195

- 2-time All-Star
- .285 career BA
- 668 career stolen bases
- Royals Hall of Fame inductee (2000)

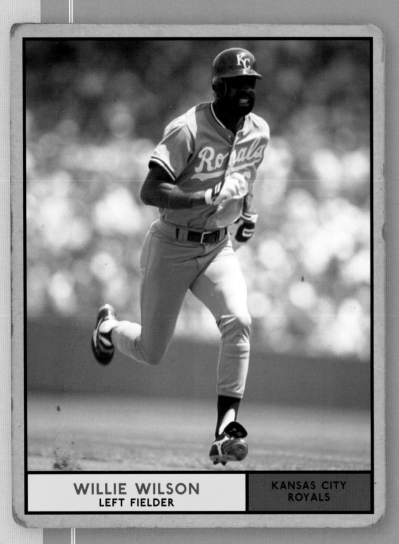

WILLIE WILSON
LEFT FIELDER

KANSAS CITY
ROYALS

A TEAM IN TRANSITION

Brett's retirement, coupled with the death of longtime team owner Ewing Kauffman, heralded a time of transition for the Kansas City Royals. After winning six division titles and one World Series, the small-market team was suddenly struggling to hold on to talented young players and remain competitive. Standout hurler David Cone did his best to help, winning 16 games in 1994. But it was obvious that the financially strapped team would have to trade the star pitcher before the next season. Kansas City's financial situation was so critical that it became one of baseball owners' favorite arguments for reorganizing the economics of baseball, which featured some teams having a payroll three times that of others. The differences in opinion between players and owners on how to achieve this change eventually led to a strike that began on August 12, 1994. At the time of the strike, Kansas City was 64–51 and in third place in the new AL Central Division.

When the players returned in April 1995, Cone was gone. In his stead, Appier and Montgomery anchored the pitching staff. First baseman Wally Joyner and third baseman Gary Gaetti led the offense and helped the team to a respectable 70–74, second in the AL Central.

A second-place finish was out of the question in 1996, though. For the first

Although 36 years old and nearing the end of his career, Gary Gaetti bopped a career-high 35 homers in 1995.

time in the team's 27-year history, Kansas City finished dead last in its division, 75–86, a full 24 games out of first place. In 1997, the Royals finished last again. In 1998, with the help of speedy outfielder Johnny Damon, who paced the team with 104 runs, the Royals managed to stay out of the cellar, but they still finished a lowly 72–89.

The 1999 season was in part a sad one—and not just because the Royals suffered yet another losing campaign. Former star Dan Quisenberry, the team's ace closer for 10 seasons, died at his home in Leawood, Kansas, of brain cancer—the same disease that had claimed the life of manager Dick Howser in 1987. But as fans remembered Quisenberry's life and career, they also had the privilege of seeing one of their own ushered into the Hall of Fame: George Brett was voted into the Hall in his first year of eligibility. "It's very, very special," Brett said at a news conference following the announcement. "When you start playing, it's a dream that you will make it, but you don't really think that dream will ever come true."

KEVIN APPIER

The other bright spot in the 1999 season was Carlos Beltran, a young center fielder who belted 22 home runs and drove in 108 runs during his rookie campaign. His impressive statistics, which earned him AL Rookie of the Year honors, were the highlight of an otherwise lackluster 64–97 season.

Even more disappointing than the string of losing records in the late '90s were the team's continued financial problems. After the 2000 season, the cash-strapped Royals were forced to trade away both Damon and Jermaine Dye, a Gold-Glove-winning outfielder who had led the team in home runs in 1999 and 2000. Although the fans were frustrated by the loss of such star

JOSE OFFERMAN – Offerman energized the Royals' offense with his speed in 1998, swiping 45 bases and ripping a league-leading 13 triples. But, like many Royals standouts of the late '90s, the second baseman then left the team for a richer contract offer elsewhere.

Versatile and hustling outfielder Johnny Damon spent his first six big-league seasons wearing Royals blue.

JOHNNY DAMON

players, Royals general manager Allard Baird insisted that the Dye deal was not based solely on economics. "We have the makings of a pretty good pitching staff in the works," he said. "Do we have some holes to fill? Yes, we do. But the bottom line is we're looking up in the standings, and we need to become a better ballclub."

YOUNG ROYALTY

hat better ballclub would take time to build. Although first baseman Mike Sweeney boasted a consistently solid average, third baseman Joe Randa had a strong swing, and Beltran had developed into a true power hitter, the rest of the team struggled. The 2002 season ended in the club's first-ever 100-loss campaign.

After such a disappointing year, no one had high hopes for the 2003 Royals. But under new manager Tony Peña, the team won its first nine games and ended April a remarkable 17–7. Although injuries slowed the team's hot pace by midseason, the incredible offensive output of rookie shortstop Angel Berroa helped the Royals stay in contention through September. Although Kansas City ultimately fell short of the playoffs, Berroa earned the Rookie of the Year award, and Peña was honored as AL Manager of the Year.

CENTER FIELDER · AMOS OTIS

For 14 years, one of the most popular chants heard in Royals Stadium was "A-O, A-O," which heralded one of Amos Otis's dazzling plays in the outfield or his appearance at the plate. Although Otis was sometimes criticized for what appeared to be a lackadaisical attitude in the outfield, he was an excellent fielder who made difficult plays appear simple, making easy one-handed catches and smooth throws to the infield. He also hustled on the base paths, stealing five bases in one game and leading the league with 52 steals in 1971. Otis retired a year after leaving the Royals.

AMOS OTIS
CENTER FIELDER

**KANSAS CITY
ROYALS**

STATS

Royals seasons: 1970–83

Height: 5-11

Weight: 166

- **5-time All-Star**

- **3-time Gold Glove winner**

- **193 career HR**

- **2,020 career hits**

RIGHT FIELDER · BO JACKSON

Bo Jackson had two choices when he finished college in 1985: play pro football for the Tampa Bay Buccaneers, or play baseball for the Kansas City Royals. He chose the Royals. But in 1987, his love of football prompted Jackson to announce that he would play for the Los Angeles Raiders as a "hobby" during baseball's off-season. Although Royals management wasn't happy, Jackson returned in 1988 to hit 25 homers—some of them monstrous blasts—and steal 27 bases. His two-sport career ended when he injured a hip playing football in 1990. He returned to baseball briefly but was forced to retire in 1994.

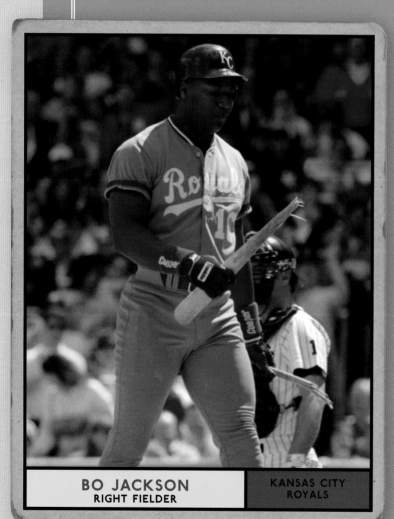

BO JACKSON
RIGHT FIELDER

KANSAS CITY
ROYALS

STATS

Royals seasons: 1986–90

Height: 6-1

Weight: 225

- **1989 All-Star Game MVP**
- **141 career HR**
- **415 career RBI**
- **82 career stolen bases**

THE ROYAL CASTLE

The Kansas City Royals play their home games in one of the most beautiful ballparks in the game—but Kauffman Stadium certainly isn't the newest. When it opened on April 10, 1973, Royals Stadium (as it was known until being renamed for owner Ewing Kauffman in 1993) was a state-of-the-art facility. It had artificial turf, distant outfield walls, and fountains just beyond the fences—a nod to Kansas City's reputation as "The City of Fountains." In the past two decades, the building has been significantly renovated and modernized. In 1990, a JumboTron display board went up in left field,

topped by the four golden prongs of the Royals crown. In 1995, the turf, which had previously been considered a home advantage for the Royals, was replaced with natural grass, and its fountains were replaced by a "water spectacular," a grand, 322-foot-wide fountain that stretches into the left-field corner. And before the 2004 season began, the outfield walls were pushed back to their original dimensions of 330 feet in left and right fields, 410 in center, and 385 in both left-center and right-center, making Kauffman Stadium one of the most spacious parks in major league baseball.

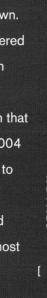

ROYALS

A ROYAL MESS

Things had been going south for the Royals
for more than a decade. The team hadn't had
a winning season since 1993, when, despite
having to trade or give up many of its best
players because of increasing salary demands,
it pulled off an 83–79 record in 2003. Hopes
were high for similar success in 2004—in
fact, many baseball experts picked the team
to win the AL Central—but the Royals ended
up sinking to a new low. They won only seven
games in all of April; by the end of May, they had
added only 10 more. To make matters worse,
it was clear that management was shopping
young star Carlos Beltran around the league,
hoping to trade the talented player before
losing him to free agency in the off-season.
On June 24, Beltran was sent to the Houston
Astros for two players and cash. The Royals
responded by losing 14 of their next 16 games.
In July, they suffered through an eight-game
losing streak, then wrapped up September and
started October by dropping another seven in
a row. By the time the season mercifully ended
on October 3, the Royals had set a franchise
record for the most losses in a season: 104.

CARLOS BELTRAN

MANAGER · DICK HOWSER

As a player, Dick Howser was a shortstop best known for his quick feet and solid swing. As a manager, he was recognized as the man who took over the Kansas City Royals in the midst of a strike-shortened 1981 season and, in four short years, turned them into world champions. While managing the AL All-Star team in 1986, broadcasters noticed him mixing up signals when he changed pitchers; two days later, he was diagnosed with a brain tumor. Howser tried to return to the dugout for the 1987 season but was too ill. He passed away three months later at the age of 51.

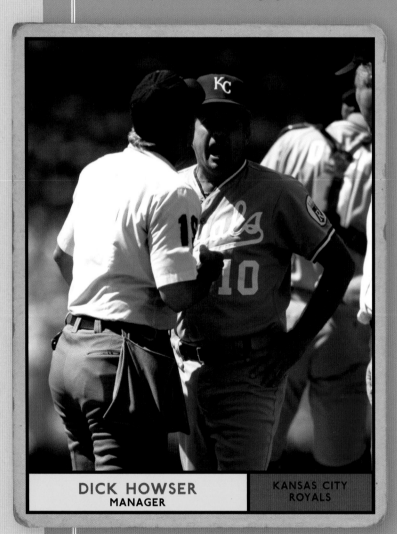

DICK HOWSER
MANAGER

KANSAS CITY
ROYALS

STATS

Royals seasons as manager: 1981–86

Height: 5-8

Weight: 155

Managerial Record: 507–425

World Series Championship: 1985

MIKE SWEENEY

MIKE SWEENEY – The Royals tried to trade Sweeney away in 1999 after he had spent four poor seasons in Kansas City. Luckily, the team found no takers, and the first baseman and designated hitter became a sharp-eyed slugger and a clubhouse leader.

On opening day of the 2004 season, the third-largest crowd in the history of Kauffman Stadium watched as Carlos Beltran hit a walk-off home run to seal a victory over the Chicago White Sox. Unfortunately, subsequent wins were few and far between. Beltran was traded away in June, and besides a record-setting 26–5 victory over the Detroit Tigers in September, there were few memorable moments. The team's 58–104 record set a new franchise mark for most losses; only the Arizona Diamondbacks, who finished 51–111, had a worse season.

The Royals showed little improvement in 2005 and 2006, topping 100 losses again each year. But heading into 2007, Kansas City fans saw glimmers of hope. The team featured proven talent in Berroa and Sweeney, and pitcher Zack Greinke seemed ready to shine. Fans were also encouraged by the 2006 signing of hurler Gil Meche and the boundless talent of Alex Gordon, a fast-rising third baseman in the club's minor-league system. "This is a new year, and I'm excited," Sweeney said as 2007 spring training began. "There's a new atmosphere in the clubhouse."

From George Brett to Angel Berroa, the Royals have a long tradition of developing talented players who have helped lead the team to the top. Although recent times have been tough in Kansas City, as the young Royals continue to mature, their heartland home waits eagerly for them to bring baseball's greatest glory—a World Series crown—back to the city.

ANGEL BERROA

Kansas City fans counted on Angel Berroa to lead the Royals up the AL Central standings in 2007 and beyond.

INDEX